STEVE JOBS AND STEVE WOZNIAK

LAURA LA BELLA

ROSEN
PUBLISHING

NEW YORK

Published in 2016 by The Rosen Publishing Group, Inc.
29 East 21st Street, New York, NY 10010

Library of Congress Cataloging-in-Publication Data

Names: La Bella, Laura, author.
Title: Steve Jobs and Steve Wozniak / Laura La Bella.
Description: First edition. | New York, NY : The Rosen Publishing Group, Inc., 2016. | Series: Tech pioneers | Audience: Grades 7-12. | Includes bibliographical references and index.
Identifiers: LCCN 2015033182 | ISBN 9781499462869 (library bound)
Subjects: LCSH: Jobs, Steve, 1955–2011—Juvenile literature. | Wozniak, Steve, 1950-—Juvenile literature. | Apple Computer, Inc.—History—Juvenile literature. | Computer engineers—United States—Biography—Juvenile literature. | Inventors—United States—Biography—Juvenile literature. | Computer industry—United States—History—Juvenile literature. | Businesspeople—United States—Biography—Juvenile literature.
Classification: LCC QA76.2.J63 L3 2016 | DDC 621.39/092—dc23

Manufactured in the United States of America.

CONTENTS

The Apple iPod changed everything about the way we listen to music. This small device made it possible for you to carry your entire music library in your pocket.

The Apple iPhone changed everything about the way we communicate. The smartphone ushered in constant, on-the-go access to the Internet and gave users unprecedented ways to connect—from text messages, e-mail, and social media to hundreds of thousands of other apps—all at your fingertips.

Though the iPod and iPhone hit the market in the mid-2000s, both products can find their origins in the early collaboration of Apple's two founders: the charismatic Steve Jobs and the intelligent, forward-thinking Steve Wozniak.

Since they became friends and began collaborating in 1971, the computing industry has never been the same. With the Apple I computer, the first personal computer to have mass-market appeal, Jobs and Wozniak altered the landscape of the computing

Steve Jobs stands in front of a vintage photo of himself and Apple cofounder Steve Wozniak on January 27, 2010, to announce the launch of Apple's iPad.

industry and redefined how and why we should use a computer. With the Apple II, they redefined who should use a computer. No longer were computers for programming hobbyists. Instead they were for everyone.

By the mid-1980s, however, both Jobs and Wozniak had moved on from Apple and began investing and developing other forms of technology. Wozniak helped to design and develop the first universal remote control and invested in several technology companies that were on the cusp of major advances in computing and innovation technology. Jobs bought a small animation studio, and with an infusion of technology and vision, Pixar Animation Studios—the studio behind *Toy Story* and other top-grossing animated films—was born.

But Apple began to suffer under the watch of others, and by the late 1990s, Jobs returned to lead the company during its most profitable stage yet. It was his vision behind the development of the iPod, a device that changed how we buy, listen to, and transport our music; the iMac, an all-in-one computer that took the guesswork out of computer setup and became the best-selling personal computer in history; and the iPhone, which changed how we communicate, stay connected, and get information on the go. Although Jobs may have become the face of Apple both in its infancy as a company and later when it began to introduce groundbreaking products, Wozniak's role as the brainpower cannot be denied. He pioneered much of the technology used in computing today and set the stage for Apple to become an internationally recognized consumer product company.

Despite differences in leadership styles, professional goals, technical abilities, and even different tenures with the company, Jobs and Wozniak's innovations, along with their maverick attitude, set the stage for the company's comeback and eventual market and cultural dominance. When Jobs died in 2011, Wozniak told the Huffington Post, "We've lost something we won't get back." He said this of Jobs's passing, but added, "the way I see it, though, the way people love products he put so much into creating means he brought a lot of life to the world."

Chapter One

A Tale of Two Steves

L ong before Steve Jobs and Steve Wozniak created Apple Computer, Inc., a company that would change the world of computing, first by introducing the personal computer and then by pioneering advanced mobile devices, the two future technology pioneers were neighborhood friends who shared a love for tinkering with electronics and playing practical jokes.

STEVE JOBS

Steven Paul Jobs was born on February 24, 1955, in San Francisco, California, and was adopted as an infant by Paul and Clara Jobs.

Jobs's biological parents, Joanne Schieble and Abdulfattah Jandali, were not married and Jandali was a Muslim Syrian immigrant. Schieble's parents, who disapproved of their daughter's relationship with Jandali, pressured the couple to give their baby boy up for adoption.

Paul and Clara Jobs, who could not have children of their own, adopted the baby, whom they named Steven Paul Jobs, and in 1960, when their son was only five years old, the Jobs family moved from San Francisco to Mountain View, California. At the time the Mountain

Silicon Valley, the southern part of the San Francisco Bay Area, includes San Jose, Alameda, Napa, and Sonoma and is home to major technology companies.

View area was just beginning to emerge as a burgeoning technology center, and Clara Jobs found employment as a payroll clerk for Varian Associates, one of the first high-tech firms to settle in the region, which eventually became known as Silicon Valley. In 1958, the Jobses adopted another child, a daughter named Patti Jobs.

DAD FUELS INTEREST IN ELECTRONICS

Jobs's father, Paul, was raised on a dairy farm in Germantown, Wisconsin. After serving in the United States Coast Guard during World War II, where he gained skills as a mechanic and carpenter, Paul returned home and turned his hobby for buying, restoring, and selling old cars into a career as a car salesman. Like his wife, Paul Jobs was also employed by a Silicon Valley company. He spent time as a machinist for a firm that made lasers. Steve Jobs described his father as a "genius with his hands." By taking apart and reassembling various electronic equipment, Paul Jobs taught his son rudimentary electronics, how to build electronic systems, and how to work with his hands.

EDUCATION AND EARLY WORK

As a young student, Steve Jobs attended Monta Loma Elementary School in Mountain View, California. Though

William Shockley Jr., an American physicist and inventor, helped invent the transistor. Shockley and other innovators made Silicon Valley a technology hub.

SILICON VALLEY: A HUB FOR INNOVATION

Home to some of the world's most innovative high-tech companies, including Google, Apple, Hewlett-Packard, Facebook, Cisco Systems, Microsoft, and Twitter, Silicon Valley is the nickname for the Santa Clara Valley, which is part of the San Francisco Bay Area in Northern California. The area originally got its nickname from the influx of silicon chip manufacturers that flooded the region in the early 1980s. It later became a hub of technology and innovation, and by the mid-1990s Internet start-up companies, like Amazon.com and eBay, established their bases of operations in the area. In addition to technology, the area is also well-known for companies that dominate the Internet or provide web-based services and for top educational institutions such as Stanford University.

school officials recommended that he skip two grades based on his successful test scores, his parents decided that Steve would skip only one grade. He attended Cupertino Junior High and Homestead High School, both in Cupertino, California. At Homestead, Steve Jobs became friends with Bill Fernandez, a neighbor who shared his interest in electronics. Bill later introduced Steve to another neighbor, Steve Wozniak, a fellow computer and electronics whiz kid.

At an early age, Jobs was influenced by innovator Edwin Land, the creator of Polaroid cameras. In his biography, *Steve Jobs* by Walter Isaacson, Jobs said, "I always thought of myself as a humanities person as a kid, but I liked electronics. Then I read something that one of my heroes, Edwin Land of Polaroid, said about the importance of people who could stand at the intersection of humanities and sciences, and I decided that's what I wanted to do."

Land played a pivotal role in helping to develop spy plane cameras during the Cold War. He was asked by President Dwight D. Eisenhower to help build U-2 spy plane cameras to assess how much of a threat the Soviet Union was to the United States in the 1950s. The film from those spy cameras was developed and analyzed at the NASA Ames Research Center, located in Sunnyvale, California, not far from where Jobs grew up. Jobs's father brought his son to the Ames Research Center to see the technology. Jobs later told Isaacson that the visit was influential. "The first computer terminal I ever saw was when my dad brought me to the Ames Center. I totally fell in love with it."

In 1972, Jobs graduated from high school and enrolled in Reed College in Portland, Oregon. After six

Edwin H. Land, inventor of the Polaroid camera and surveillance technology during the Cold War, was an early influence on Steve Jobs.

months, he dropped out and spent time traveling through India, where he gained an appreciation for the Buddhist religion. When he returned to the United States, Jobs began working at Atari, a video game development company. There he created circuit boards for Breakout, one of Atari's arcade games. He also reconnected with Steve Wozniak, who was in the midst of designing and developing a personal computer.

PERSONAL LIFE

Jobs's biological parents, Joanne Schieble and Abdulfattah Jandali, eventually married, and in 1957, they had another child, a daughter named Mona Simpson. In his twenties, Jobs discovered that he had a biological sister and the two maintained a close relationship until Jobs's death in 2011.

In 1978, Jobs and his girlfriend at the time, Chrisann Brennan, had a daughter, whom they named Lisa Brennan-Jobs. In 1989, Jobs met his wife, Laurene Powell, at Stanford Business School. Jobs had been invited to the school to give a speech and he happened to be seated next to Powell, who was then studying for an MBA at the school. "I looked to my right, and there was a beautiful girl there, so we started chatting a bit while I was waiting to be introduced," Jobs said in his biography. In 1991, Jobs married Powell in a Buddhist ceremony in Yosemite

National Park. They had three children together: Reed Jobs, born in 1991; Erin Jobs, born in 1995; and Eve Jobs, born in 1998.

STEVE WOZNIAK

Stephen Gary Wozniak was born on August 11, 1950, in San Jose, California. At the time, the city of San Jose was becoming a growing epicenter for technology, and key companies in the electronics industry were beginning to establish their roots in the region. Wozniak's father, Jacob Francis "Jerry" Wozniak, was an engineer at Lockheed Missiles & Space, a division of Lockheed Martin, an advanced technology company specializing in aerospace, defense, and security. His mother, Margaret Elaine Kern, was an activist for women's issues and worked on political

campaigns. Wozniak credits his mother for his liberal values. At the time of her death, Wozniak told the *San Jose Mercury News* that his mother "was always there to help. She stood up for honest and caring people."

Growing up, the energy and innovation in the San Jose area fueled Wozniak's natural curiosity for

Steve Jobs worked at Atari, creator of the Atari 2600 video gaming system in 1977. Jobs designed the circuit board for a video game called *Breakout*.

electronics. Wozniak and Bill Fernandez grew up in a neighborhood filled with engineers, computer programmers, and other professionals who held technical jobs. They were all employed at the local tech firms, like Hewlett-Packard, Lockheed, General Electric, and Fairchild Semiconductor, or at the NASA Ames Research Center. Many of these engineers were also hobbyists who tinkered with electronics at home and had personal workshops in their garages.

As a kid, Wozniak built homemade gadgets like a voltmeter, a ham radio, calculators, and gaming devices. He credits his father and his teachers for supporting and encouraging his interest in technology. In an interview with the *San Jose Mercury News* Wozniak said, "My 4th and 5th grade teacher was a real inspiration to me—just that she seemed to care about students so much. It was

at the time that my other hero, my father, was teaching me the values of education—why children have to learn to make this a better world than the parents had made and why school is so important to your life. I

Steve Wozniak began his career working at Hewlett-Packard designing scientific calculators similar to this HP 9810A, the first programmable desktop calculator.

decided I wanted to be an engineer like my father, and second, I wanted to be a 5th grade teacher."

It was around the fourth grade when Wozniak read *Tom Swift*, a series of children's science fiction and adventure novels featuring a young scientific inventor. Wozniak felt inspired by the books. He told the *San Jose Mercury News* that the books "were about this young guy who was an engineer who could design anything, and he owned his own company, and he would entrap aliens, and build submarines, and have projects all over the world. It was just the most intriguing world."

Wozniak had a group of like-minded friends who were all into electronics. In an interview with the *San Jose Mercury News*, he said his knowledge of computing and electronics was all self-taught: "I didn't ever take a course, didn't ever buy a book on how to do it. Just pieced it together in my own head. I loved doing it, because when we were in elementary school and junior high school and even high school, it was neat to have other friends in electronics down the block. We would run house-to-house wired intercoms and somebody would build a neat little sound maker, and we'd go down to Sunnyvale Electronics and buy the parts. It was neat to grow up with a crowd of electronics kids. That was a big part of my life. That was how we had our fun."

With Fernandez, Wozniak built his first computer, which they called the Cream Soda Computer, named for the soda that the two drank while they designed and built the computer.

EDUCATION AND EARLY CAREER

Wozniak showed a special aptitude for learning, especially anything having to do with electronics. He designed and built a number of computers during his teens and won an award for building a binary adding and subtracting machine, one of a number of small computers and devices he built by hand. While he was a student at Cupertino Junior High School, Wozniak won an award for the best electronics project at the Bay Area Science Fair. He attended Homestead High School and his teachers found him to be too advanced for the electronics and math courses the school was offering. He won several awards for his achievements in math and electronics. He also began to attend seminars at the University of Santa Clara to learn more about electronics, engineering, and math.

Although Wozniak was very smart and did well in his classes, he hated the traditional school structure. He was accepted to and enrolled at the University of Colorado in 1968 but later dropped out. He then attended the University of California at Berkeley but took a leave of absence to work for Hewlett-Packard, where he began designing engineering calculators. It was at Hewlett-Packard that Wozniak got the idea for the personal computer. At an event at Georgia State University in February 2013, Wozniak told a crowd of students that his work on a personal computing device happened at night and on the weekends. "When I finished designing calculators at HP in the daytime, I went home, watched Star Trek and then [worked on his computer projects]." Wozniak developed and designed the hardware, circuit boards, and operating system that would eventually become the Apple I, the world's first personal computer. Wozniak brought his project to his bosses at Hewlett-Packard. "I begged [HP] to make the [Apple I]," he told the crowd. "Five times they turned me down."

In 1986, after Wozniak left Apple, he finally completed his college education and earned an undergraduate degree in electrical engineering and computer science. In an article in the *Los Angeles Times*, Wozniak explained that he didn't exactly drop out of UC Berkeley. "I simply took a year off to earn money for my fourth year of school. And then my career kept going up," he said.

PERSONAL LIFE

Wozniak married Candice Clark in June 1981. Clark worked for Apple as a financial analysis staffer and was a member of the 1976 U.S. Olympic canoeing team.

Together Wozniak and Clark had three children: Jesse, Sara, and Gary. The couple divorced in 1987. In 2008, Wozniak married Janet Hill, an Apple education development executive.

AN INTRODUCTION CHANGES THE WORLD OF COMPUTING

In 1971, Bill Fernandez was walking around his neighborhood with his friend Steve Jobs when the two saw Steve Wozniak washing his car. Fernandez thought his two friends, who were both highly technical and loved dabbling in electronics, would hit it off. So he introduced Jobs to Wozniak. In 2007, in an interview with *PC World*, Wozniak talked about meeting Jobs for the first time. "We first met during my college years, while he was in high school. It was 1971 when a friend said, you should meet Steve Jobs, because he likes electronics and he also plays pranks. So he introduced us. We both loved electronics and the way we used to hook up digital chips. Very few people, especially back then, had any idea what chips were, how they worked and what they could do," he said.

Soon, Wozniak and Jobs began working together on various electronics projects. When Wozniak showed Jobs the hardware for the Apple I computer, it was Jobs who recognized its potential. In the Apple I, Wozniak integrated a number of technologies and combined components no one else was doing at the time. It was also designed with significantly fewer parts than existing computers. Wozniak wrote in his autobiography that the Apple I was "the first low-cost computer which, out of the box, you didn't have to be a geek to use."

Chapter Two

A Friendship Leads to a Business

While Steve Wozniak and Steve Jobs both were employed elsewhere—Jobs at Atari and Wozniak at Hewlett-Packard—they began working together on Wozniak's design for a personal computer. Wozniak had offered up the idea to his bosses at Hewlett-Packard, who turned him down. But Jobs recognized the potential in Wozniak's project and eventually talked Wozniak into starting their own computer company.

THE LAUNCH OF APPLE COMPUTER, INC.

In an interview with the *San Jose Mercury News*, Wozniak recalled the moment he and Jobs decided to launch a business. He told the newspaper that Jobs "saw [the computer] and said: 'Why don't we make a PC board?' Basically it was like a $1,000 investment and we'd have to sell fifty to get our money back, because we'd build the boards for $20 and sell them for $40. And boy, I remember not being sure we'd sell fifty of them. But, you know, Steve thought there were surplus dealers and all that. And then finally he said, 'Even if we lose our money, at least we had a company.'" Originally Wozniak and Jobs wanted to pitch their invention, the Apple I, to computer science hobbyists, not to the general public.

Steve Jobs's childhood home in Los Altos, California, is still owned by the Jobs family and remains a destination for fans and tourists.

Wozniak knew in the moment that they were on the cusp of a major moment in computing history. He told *Bloomberg Business*:

I was totally aware that a revolution was close to starting, that pretty soon we were going to have computers that were affordable. Every computer before the Apple I looked like—you have to imagine the most awful, not understandable computer you've ever seen in a museum or in a new movie. That's what they all looked like. They had these big front panels of metal switches and lights and stuff, and nobody could understand them except a computer expert. The Apple I was the first one to have a keyboard and a video display. A television. You would type on the keyboard and see your words on the television, or the computer could type its own words on the television and play games with you and ask questions and give answers. That was a turning point in history.

Wozniak and Jobs showed the Apple I to the members of the Homebrew Computer Club, an early computer hobbyist group that met regularly in the Silicon Valley area to trade parts and talk about building computers and computing devices. Paul Terrell, an early member of the club, established the Byte Shop, one of the first retailers of the personal computer. Upon seeing Wozniak and Jobs's

Apple Computer's first product, the Apple I, was introduced in 1977 and sold for $666. Fifty were made and, to date, only six are known to still work.

presentation of the Apple I at the meeting, Terrell bought the first fifty Apple I computers. According to Jobs's biography, Terrell wanted the computers fully assembled. At the time computers were available as kits, which was how Wozniak and Jobs had intended to sell the Apple I, but Terrell was having trouble selling kits since customers found the assembly too difficult. So Terrell offered Wozniak and Jobs $500 for each assembled computer they delivered. The Apple I became the first personal computer to be manufactured and sold as a completely assembled unit.

When Wozniak and Jobs realized they needed technical help, they turned to their friend Bill Fernandez, who became one of Apple's first employees. Wozniak said in an interview with the TechRepublic, "Bill was really in that early circle of founders at Apple. He was part of the family." Fernandez says that this time, at the very beginning of Apple as the three of them were getting their feet wet running a company, was an incredible adventure and he could tell they were on to something big. He told TechRepublic, "There was magic in the air. There was also this implication that we were going to change the world, or we were going to change society in a significant way . . . that we were empowering ordinary people to do things unimaginable, that we were putting the latent, potential power of technology into the hands of the people."

Wozniak and Jobs, along with Ronald Wayne, an early investor, founded Apple Computer, Inc., on April 1, 1976, to sell the Apple I computers to Terrell. The company was incorporated on January 3, 1977, but without Wayne on board, who in July 1976 sold his shares of Apple back to Wozniak and Jobs. With the success of the Apple I, Wozniak began to develop his next computer system, the Apple II, which had the ability to display color graphics and had BASIC, a programming language, built into its operating system. The Apple II was introduced to consumers on April 16, 1977, at the first West Coast Computer Faire, an annual computer industry conference at which computer companies could

THE MYTH OF WHERE APPLE STARTED

One address—2066 Crist Drive in Los Altos, California— is famous among die-hard fans of Apple computers and those who aspire to the greatness of Steve Jobs, one of the company's cofounders. But Steve Wozniak, cofounder of Apple Computers and chief designer of its two pioneering computers, the Apple I and the Apple II, says the garage was just a place to call home for its founders. "The garage is a bit of a myth," Wozniak told *Bloomberg Business.* "We did no designs there, no breadboarding, no prototyping, no planning of products. We did no manufacturing there." That hasn't stopped fans from traveling to Jobs's childhood home to pay homage to Apple's creators. The home, which is occupied by Jobs's stepmother and owned by the Jobs Trust, was named a historic site in 2013 by the Los Altos Historic Commission.

Although the public regards the Jobs family garage as the place where Apple began, there were other tech start-ups that really did begin in garages. Several major companies found their origins in garages, including tech powerhouses like Hewlett-Packard, Google, Microsoft, Amazon.com, and even entertainment giant Disney.

show off their latest products. The internal components of the Apple II were completely different from the Apple I. It had a redesigned TV interface, which could display simple text as well as graphics and color. The Apple II was soon chosen as the best computer for use in the business world and sales took off.

With Apple Computer taking off, Wozniak resigned from his job at Hewlett-Packard and became vice president in charge of research and development at Apple. Jobs quit his job as a technician at Atari to work full-time at Apple, though he did not have a formal title at Apple until the mid-1980s, when he was named chairman of the board.

There were a few early investors in Apple Computer, among them Mike Markkula, who also became the company's second CEO.

ANOTHER LANDMARK CREATION IS LAUNCHED

As the Apple III was being developed, another team of developers, headed by Jobs, was designing the Lisa, Apple's first graphical user interface, or GUI, computer. It was

the computer that would introduce new words—such as mouse, desktop, icon, and lexicon—into the computer world, and it all began with a trip to Xerox PARC.

In exchange for $1 million of Apple stock, given to them prior to the launch of Apple's stock to the public, Xerox gave Jobs, Wozniak, and other Apple engineers three days of access to Xerox's PARC facilities. PARC, which stood for Palo Alto Research Center, was Xerox's research and development center. PARC is responsi-

Steve Wozniak attends the West Coast Computer Faire, where the Apple II was introduced.

ble for developing a number of innovative products or processes, including laser printing, Ethernet, and object-oriented programming. After visiting PARC, the Apple staff walked away with a number of ideas that would eventually be incorporated into the design for the Lisa.

The Apple III was the first Apple machine to feature a built-in floppy disk drive and high-resolution graphics, but it was plagued by problems and did not sell well.

The Lisa introduced the mouse, which navigated a desktop where folders and icons assisted with organizing files of documents. It was the first time computers had used such innovation in their design and presentation of information to the user. But sales of the Lisa were poor. Jobs was taken off Apple's Lisa project and instead assigned to the Macintosh project.

The Lisa was groundbreaking for the computer industry, but the unit, priced at nearly $10,000, was too expensive and only around one hundred thousand of them were sold, mostly to businesses.

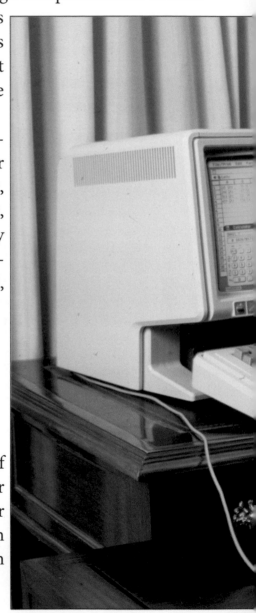

CHANGES BRING ABOUT DEPARTURES

During the first five years of its operations, revenue for Apple doubled every four months, an average growth rate of 700 percent. With

growth came the introduction of more products, including the Apple III, the Lisa, and the Macintosh.

On December 12, 1980, Apple went public at $22
a share, generating more capital than any initial pub-

Steve Jobs debuts the new Lisa computer at a press
conference in 1983. Lisa was groundbreaking, but at
$10,000, it was too expensive for the general public.

35

lic offering, or IPO, since the Ford Motor Company's in 1956. Going from a private to a public company generated millions of dollars, which was capital Apple Computer needed to launch additional products. It also made Wozniak and Jobs instant millionaires.

In 1981, Wozniak was involved in a plane crash that left him with serious injuries. He took a leave of absence from Apple to recover. During his absence, significant changes occurred at Apple.

It was in 1984, when Apple launched the Macintosh, that the company became a sensation. The Macintosh was the first personal computer to be sold without a programming language. Apple's launch of its new product was groundbreaking. Apple aired a commercial, titled "1984," during the Super Bowl to announce that a revolution was about to happen in the computing industry. Later that year, in November, Apple bought all thirty-nine pages of advertising in *Newsweek* magazine to promote the Macintosh computer. The "Test Drive a Macintosh" promotion allowed a customer with a credit card to take a Macintosh computer home for twenty-four hours to give it a test run.

While the company was enjoying success, some internal struggles were becoming an issue for Wozniak and Jobs. Jobs had recruited John Sculley, the former president of Pepsi-Cola, to join Apple as its chief executive officer. An expert in marketing, Jobs wanted

"1984" COMMERCIAL PUTS APPLE ON THE MAP

Widely recognized as the greatest commercial in Super Bowl commercial history, "1984," Apple's first advertisement to launch the Macintosh computer, was aired in the third quarter of the game. Ridley Scott, known for directing several Hollywood blockbuster films, including *Alien* and *Blade Runner*, directed the commercial. The commercial, with its alluring message about the promise and impact of technology, resonated with consumers, who flooded electronics stores the following Tuesday when the Macintosh computer was released for sale.

Sculley to help Apple brand itself. Sculley was put in charge of marketing while Jobs retained the title of chairman of the board, informally leading the company's product development.

When the Macintosh was released for sale, Sculley raised the price from $1,995 to $2,495. His reasoning was that the company needed to raise money for expensive marketing campaigns and to make a greater profit off the Macintosh. Although the computer sold well, it did not have the impact Apple was

In 1984, Steve Jobs recruited John Sculley, a marketing expert, as Apple's new president. It was Jobs's hope that Sculley could help Apple with branding itself.

hoping for. As a result, Sculley cut back on Jobs's product development groups and all new projects were scrutinized for their usefulness, their cost to manufacture, and their marketability.

Sculley and Jobs began to disagree on business decisions and the board of directors asked Sculley to help contain Jobs, who was calling for long meetings and was attempting to launch products that had not been tested and approved by the company. Sculley tried to limit Jobs's responsibilities, but instead Jobs tried to get Sculley fired from Apple. When Sculley learned of Jobs's intentions, he called a meeting with the board of directors and informed them of Jobs's behavior and actions. The board sided with Sculley and Jobs was removed from his duties at Apple. Shortly after, Jobs resigned from Apple and no longer had any involvement in the company he helped found.

Sculley would later say in interviews that he wished Jobs had stayed on at Apple or come back to the company sooner. He told *Inc.* magazine, "Even though he was young, the reality was I will always regret that I didn't try to bring Steve back into Apple, because, unquestionably, he turned out to be the world's greatest CEO," he said.

After Jobs left, Apple found success in numerous product launches. It introduced a faster microprocessor and launched desktop publishing. It also introduced the PowerBook, Apple's laptop computer, which found success and brought in profits to the company. But by 1993, Sculley had made several mistakes and the board fired him. The company struggled for several years. It wasn't until Jobs returned to the company in 1997, with a different leadership style and a host of new ideas, that Apple found itself on top of the computer industry again.

Chapter Three

Departure from Apple

Changes in the leadership of Apple Computer began in 1981, when Wozniak was injured in a plane crash, and culminated in 1986, when Jobs was forced from the company. Both men eventually moved on from Apple, for a variety of personal and professional reasons, and went on to launch new ventures and find success in other areas of computing, and in new businesses too, such as animated movies.

Wozniak Injured in a Plane Crash

In 1981, Apple was firmly established as a player in the world of computing. The company even defined personal computing and made it possible for those interested in computers,

In the mid-1980s, Jobs was fired because of creative differences with then-president Sculley, and Wozniak reduced his involvement in the company.

but without the knowledge of a programmer or hobbyist, to enjoy the benefits of a computer at home. But the early to mid-1980s also ushered in a time of change and upheaval at Apple as Wozniak and Jobs both encountered obstacles that led to their eventual departures from the company.

On February 7, 1981, a Beechcraft Bonanza airplane Wozniak was piloting crashed soon after takeoff from the Sky Park Airport in Scotts Valley, California. Wozniak, Candice Clark, his then-fiancée, and Clark's brother and his girlfriend were on board. The two couples were departing for San Diego, California, where Wozniak and Clark were to pick up their wedding rings, when the accident happened. The plane stalled while climbing after takeoff, then bounced down the runway, crashed through two fences, and hit an embankment. Candice Clark suffered a skull fracture, numerous broken bones in her face, and a shattered finger. Wozniak suffered head trauma and broken bones and endured five weeks of anterograde amnesia, which affects the brain's ability to process new memories. Wozniak took a leave of absence from Apple to focus on his recovery. Four months after the crash, he and Clark married.

Steve Wozniak suffered head injuries, broken bones, and several weeks of amnesia after a plane crash. He took a leave of absence from Apple to recover.

Wozniak later said in interviews that Apple had become a much larger company than he had envisioned and he missed being able to tinker with electronics. The accident marked the beginning of Wozniak phasing himself out of his involvement with Apple. In 1983, when he felt he had recovered enough to go back to work, Wozniak returned to Apple and worked on product development, but by early 1987, Wozniak decided he didn't want to work for Apple on a full-time basis anymore. He said in an interview with InfoWorld that, in his opinion, Apple had "been going in the wrong direction for the last five years." Wozniak felt the company had grown too big and had lost much of the camaraderie he liked so much when the

company was smaller and employed fewer people. He told TechHive that, "being the sort of designer I was, I was designing things all on my own, working alone, and now the company grew to a point that it had organized engineering departments. I could still hang around and do any project I felt like, but I wanted to do real things with people in order to change the world and bring new products."

Wozniak never formally left Apple and remains an Apple employee to this day. "I never left being employed at Apple," he told TechHive. "Up to this day I still get a small paycheck to settle royalties."

WOZNIAK'S LIFE AFTER APPLE

In the years after he left Apple, Wozniak has spent much of his time and money identifying and investing in the next big thing in the computing and technology innovation industries. He has launched a number of different businesses, each with varying degrees of success. His first new business venture was a company called CL-9.

CL-9 was the company that developed the first universal remote control. In the mid-1980s, VCRs were gaining popularity and consumers now had to use multiple remote controls to manage both their TVs and VCRs. CL-9 created a solution: one remote control that you could program to control both your TV and VCR. Wozniak developed the idea when, with multiple electronic entertainment devices in his own home, he grew frustrated always having to reach for a new remote control to change a channel, pause the VCR, play music

from the stereo, or fast-forward a laser disk. The company invested time and money designing a remote control. They succeeded in creating one that worked, but its biggest problem was that once it was programmed, the functions of the buttons were hard to remember, making usability difficult for consumers.

After leaving Apple, Steve Wozniak became involved in numerous ventures, all centering around his interests in technology, product development, and education.

45

In 2001, Wozniak founded Wheels of Zeus (nick-named WOZ), to create wireless GPS technology. His hope was to create a compact, inexpensive GPS, or global positioning system, for consumers. Though the cell phone company Motorola got involved with Wheels of Zeus, Motorola never implemented any of the company's technology. In 2006, Wheels of Zeus was closed and Wozniak moved on. He founded Acquicor Technology, a holding for acquiring technology companies and helping to develop them. It was founded by Wozniak and two former Apple executives. Gilbert Amelio was a former chief executive at Apple, and Ellen Hancock was chief technology officer. In September 2006, Acquicor acquired Jazz Semiconductor, and Acquicor adopted Jazz Semiconductor as its own name. Jazz is a manufacturer of silicon wafers for the semiconductor industry.

In September 2007, Wozniak joined Scottevest as an advisory board member. Scottevest is a clothing company that specializes in garments with conduit systems and specialized pockets and compartments for holding mobile phones, tablets, and other portable electronic devices.

In February 2009, Wozniak joined Fusion-io, a data storage and server company, as its chief scientist. Fusion-io was named by *Businessweek* magazine as the "No. 1 innovation up-and-comer in the world."

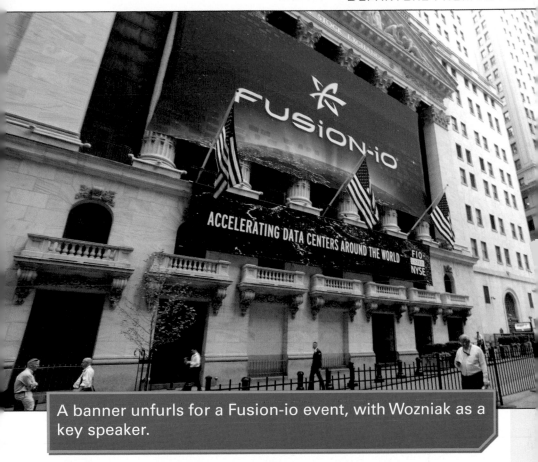

A banner unfurls for a Fusion-io event, with Wozniak as a key speaker.

AN IN-DEMAND SPEAKER

Wozniak has also become a popular speaker at a variety of events. Among the events at which he has spoken include those at business schools and technology conferences. A sample of his speaking engagements includes:

- On November 18, 2010, Wozniak gave a speech at the Science & Technology Summit at the World Forum Convention Center in The Hague.

- On October 20, 2011, Wozniak delivered a keynote presentation titled "Today's Science Fiction, Tomorrow's Science Fact" at IP EXPO, a computer expo that took place at Earls Court Exhibition Centre in London, England.
- On November 14, 2011, Wozniak was the keynote speaker at Rutgers Entrepreneurship Day at Rutgers University in New Brunswick, New Jersey.
- On May 16, 2012, Wozniak spoke at the WOZ Live event at the Melbourne Exhibition and Convention Centre in Australia.
- On October 20, 2012, Wozniak spoke at the Tijuana Innovadora event at the Tijuana Cultural Center in Tijuana, Mexico.
- On November 13, 2013, Wozniak was the keynote speaker at the Internet Summit in Raleigh, North Carolina.

BEST ADVICE FROM STEVE WOZNIAK

At conferences and in interviews, Wozniak has doled out advice to a wide variety of people, from young kids and college students to entrepreneurs and future tech pioneers. Here are some of his best pieces of advice:

"The best education comes from things you do on your own for your own reasons, not for grades. And . . .

the best thinking often comes from quiet thinking—the type done by shy kids who don't shout out correct answers first."

"Engineers at the bottom are sometimes very important. They're the heads that have the ideas that might drive your company."

"I really urge you not to think you can start a whole company and business with just ideas on paper, because you'll end up owning so few of those ideas. You have to create a working model, something that you can show people and demonstrate that it works, and then you can start building a future for it."

"Whatever develops your skills—you did certain things in your life that prepared you well, that gave you an open mind, and you should stay closely connected to the technology when you start your company."

"I just believe that the way that young people's minds develop is fascinating. If you are doing something for a grade or salary or a reward, it doesn't have as much meaning as creating something for yourself and your own life."

"Your first projects aren't the greatest things in the world, and they may have no money value, they may go nowhere, but that is how you learn—you put so much effort into making something right if it is for yourself."

A DEDICATION TO EDUCATION

Wozniak has always had an interest in education and as early as his years in elementary school wanted to become a teacher. He has a deep appreciation for teachers and the role they play in students' lives, due in large part to the influence teachers had on him growing up.

Since 1990, Wozniak has had a regular job teaching computer classes to fifth through eighth graders in the Los Gatos, California, school district. Although he does not have his teaching certification, a requirement for professional teachers, he volunteers his time and receives no compensation, or salary, for his efforts. He has worked for the district since 1990. This is his vocation, and he prepares diligently for his classes, working with former students to script the lessons.

Wozniak's interest in education also extends to a robotics competition called FIRST. "FIRST" stands for "For Inspiration and Recognition of Science and Technology." The organization operates the FIRST Robotics Competition, FIRST LEGO League, Junior FIRST LEGO League, and FIRST Tech Challenge competitions. The organization's goal is to develop ways to inspire students in engineering and technology fields. In March 2006, Wozniak attended the FIRST National Competition in Atlanta to show off Lego robots. He has since been a judge at several of the larger FIRST competitions, including the

Wozniak volunteers as a public school computer teacher in Los Gatos, California. He has also donated computers and other equipment to help students in need.

Boston FIRST Robotics Competition, where more than one thousand teams compete.

In 2014, Wozniak became an adjunct professor in the Faculty of Engineering & Information Technology at the University of Technology, Sydney, Australia.

TENSIONS RISE AT APPLE

Though Wozniak and Jobs remained friends throughout their time at Apple, and even as both went their separate

51

ways, Wozniak recognizes how difficult Jobs was to work for. He told the *Guardian* in an interview that "some of my very best friends in Apple, the most creative people in Apple who worked on the Macintosh, almost all of them said they would never, ever work for Steve Jobs again." Wozniak said he and Jobs spoke on a regular basis after they both left Apple and until Jobs's death in 2011, but rarely did they talk about technology. "Near his death, he was calling and talking about the old days, and how much fun it was, and did we ever think it was going to get this far?" he told the *Guardian*.

It was his difficult attitude that spelled the end for Jobs's first tenure with the company he helped found. In a speech Jobs gave at Stanford University in 2005, Jobs reflected on his being fired from Apple and said it was the best thing that could have happened to him: "The heaviness of being successful was replaced by the lightness of being a beginner again, less sure about everything. It freed me to enter one of the most creative periods of my life."

POWER STRUGGLE OUSTS JOBS

At the beginning of their working relationship, John Sculley, Apple's new chief executive officer (CEO), got along well with Jobs, who had personally recruited Sculley to join Apple. Sculley had been the head of marketing for Pepsi-Cola and under his tenure had launched several influential marketing campaigns that led to remarkable sales for Pepsi. Jobs had sought out the marketing expert to help market computers and Apple was hoping Sculley could keep the company working well until Jobs could create and introduce the Macintosh computer.

Sculley, in an interview with AppleInsider, said that at first the two got along great. "[Jobs] and I spent months together getting to know one another, probably almost five months. Weekends. I'd go to California, he'd come to New York, and so forth. And in those discussions, I was trying to teach him what I had learned at Pepsi about marketing," Sculley told the website. "One of the key insights we learned was that you don't sell the product, you sell the experience."

Things were going well between the two until the Macintosh Office failed to sell. "The Macintosh sales were not doing well and Steve and I started to have major disagreements on what we should do about it. Steve wanted to lower the price of the Macintosh. And yet he still wanted to run substantial advertising behind the product," he told AppleInsider. Sculley, with his business knowledge, said Apple needed to establish expectations for sales and profits and had a responsibility to shareholders, as a public company, to have a business plan in place. The board agreed with Sculley and asked Jobs to step down from leading the Macintosh division.

According to Jobs's biography, Apple offered Jobs a new role within the company. They wanted him to become a global product visionary, which would enable Jobs with work with a number of smaller development groups throughout Apple to design and develop

Steve Jobs gives an interview at the headquarters of NeXT in Redwood City, California.

new products. Jobs thought about the offer for several months before deciding against the idea and ultimately quitting Apple.

When Jobs spoke of the experience of being ousted from his own company at Stanford Business School in 2005, he said, "I'm pretty sure none of this would have happened if I hadn't been fired from Apple. It was awful-tasting medicine, but I guess the patient needed it."

Jobs left Apple and took five senior people working with small teams to develop new products with him. Together they started a new company, called NeXT.

Chapter Four

JOBS AND APPLE'S COMEBACK

After Apple, Jobs was looking for his next venture. He found it in two places: with his new venture, NeXT, and in the newly expanding and innovative field of computer animation.

NeXT was a computing company focused on making hardware and software for business and educational purposes. Though not a big success, NeXT was influential. Tim Berners-Lee, who created the Internet, used a NeXTcube workstation to develop the foundations of the first web server and web browser software. Jobs eventually sold NeXT to Apple, and some of NeXT's operating system was used as a basis for the Mac OS X operating system.

ANIMATED FILMS: A NEW DIRECTION FOR JOBS

In 1986, Jobs paid Hollywood filmmaker George Lucas, a film director and producer best known for creating the Star Wars and Indiana Jones film franchises, more than $10 million to acquire Lucasfilm's Computer Division, the computer graphics and animation division of Lucasfilm Ltd. The Computer Division was creating groundbreaking technology for animated films, such as complex flexible characters, hand-painted textures, and motion blur.

Jobs took Lucasfilm's Computer Division and formed a new company, called Pixar Animation Studios. The studio's first film under Jobs was Luxo Jr., which became the first three-dimensional computer-animated film to be nominated for an Academy Award for Best Animated Short Film. After a string of short animated films debuted, which allowed the Pixar team to create and master a number of new computer graphics styles, animation techniques, and production processes, Pixar and Disney teamed up and agreed to create and distribute at least one animated movie. That movie was *Toy Story*.

In 1995, *Toy Story* was released and became a big hit with audiences. Tom Hanks and Tim Allen, two of the biggest movie and television actors of the 1990s, lent their voices to the movie's two lead characters. Several

Pixar became a household name after releasing *Toy Story* and went on to release popular animated films that cemented its reputation as a pioneer in film and graphics.

other popular actors also voiced minor characters. *Toy Story* was the world's first computer-animated feature film. It was the highest-grossing film of 1995, making $192 million in the United States and more than $362 million internationally. The film was also nominated for several Academy Awards, including for Best Original Song, Best Original Score, and Best Original Screenplay.

Jobs's investment in computer animation continued to pay off when Pixar and Disney announced a joint partnership to produce five films over a ten-year period.

Several of those films—including *A Bug's Life, Toy Story 2, For the Birds, Monsters, Inc., Finding Nemo,* and *The Incredibles*—would go on to become top-grossing films, breaking box-office attendance records and winning multiple Academy Awards.

In 2006, Disney announced that it would buy Pixar in a deal worth $7.4 billion. At the time of the deal, Jobs said in a statement that with the merger "Disney and Pixar can now collaborate without the barriers that come from two different companies with two different sets of shareholders. Now, everyone can focus on what is most important, creating innovative stories, characters and films that delight millions of people around the world." As part of the deal, Jobs became a board member at Disney and also became Disney's largest individual shareholder.

JOBS RETURNS TO APPLE

In 1997, at the same time that Jobs was spearheading Pixar and helping to create innovative animation processes that would change how animated films were created and produced, Apple Computer was operating at a loss. Its biggest competitor, Microsoft, was gaining in popularity, and consumers were purchasing its Windows 95 operating system in high volumes. Members of the board of directors at Apple decided they needed to return to the

Steve Jobs returned to Apple in the late 1990s and launched an impressive array of new products that forever changed the technology landscape.

maverick style of leadership that had helped establish the company under Jobs and Wozniak. They asked Jobs to rejoin the board.

Jobs took on the role of interim CEO due to his involvement with Pixar and his growing family. At the time, Jobs and his wife, Laurene Powell Jobs, had two small children and a third was due to be born in 1998. In August 1998, Jobs rededicated himself to Apple and became chief executive officer.

One of the first things Jobs did as CEO was to establish a partnership between Apple and Microsoft. At the 1997 Macworld Expo, Jobs announced the deal, which was a five-year commitment from Microsoft to release Microsoft Office for Macintosh as well as a $150 million investment in Apple. At the expo, Jobs said:

> If we want to move forward and see Apple healthy and prospering again, we have to let go of a few things here. We have to let go of this notion that for Apple to win, Microsoft has to lose. We have to embrace a notion that for Apple to win, Apple has to do a really good job . . . So, the era of setting this up as a competition between Apple and Microsoft is over as far as I'm concerned. This is about getting Apple healthy, this is about Apple being able to make incredibly great contributions to the industry and to get healthy and prosper again.

THE MACWORLD EXPO

The Macworld Expo was first launched in 1985 in San Francisco. At first, it was the world's largest collection of Mac users gathering to discuss products. Before the Internet was invented, Macworld was the place to see and play with Apple products, learn about the newest software, and even buy extras for your Mac computers.

At the Macworld Expo, Steve Jobs shows off the iMac, an all-in-one computer that incorporated the hard drive and the monitor into one component.

In 1997, when Jobs returned to Apple, Macworld became the place to be to learn about new Apple products and to hear Jobs himself talk about the company, its successes, its direction, and its future. It was at Macworld that Apple announced the launch of such revolutionary products as the iPod, the iMac, the iPhone, and the iPad.

In 2009, Apple announced that it would no longer participate in Macworld, saying that consumers could get a similar experience at an Apple store instead. It was announced in October 2014 that Macworld would be going on a hiatus, with no annual event scheduled for 2015. The event's organizers said that in today's world of learning in front of your computer and even watching live streaming events, an expo that featured hands-on training and demos might no longer be needed.

The second thing he did was assess the current computing industry to see where opportunities lay for Apple to succeed. Jobs said that computing companies like Microsoft, Dell, and Intel would not be able to swiftly move into designing and producing personal media and communication devices, like the iPod and the iMac. Jobs understood that Apple had the chance to introduce new technologies via devices like the iPod and iMac that these other companies could not immediately respond to, which made Apple the only product company from which consumers could buy.

APPLE BREAKS NEW GROUND

When Jobs returned to Apple, he began to lead a remarkable revolution in product design and function, which became part of his new corporate philosophy of recognizable products and simple design. At the time, Jonathan Ive was Apple's lead designer, and upon meeting Jobs, Ive thought his job with Apple was done. But instead, Jobs immediately liked Ive. Jobs would later tell Brent Schlender, who was writing a book about Jobs, that he "liked [Ive] right away. And I could tell after that first meeting that [former Apple CEO Gil Amelio] had wasted [Ive's] talent."

Jobs and Ive collaborated on the new look and design of Apple's products. Both were fans of minimal, sleek designs that were beautiful but highly functional. Jobs told Isaacson for his biography that Ive "has more operational power than anyone else at Apple except me."

Ive said in an interview with *Time* magazine that he and Jobs both shared a similar vision for perfection in their devices. "Steve and I spent months and months working on a part of a product that, often, nobody would ever see, nor realize was there. It didn't make any difference functionally. We did it because we cared, because when you realize how well you can make something, falling short, whether seen or not, feels like failure."

Jobs and Ive worked well together, with Ive describing Jobs as "easygoing," a descriptor very few people, if anyone, would ever use. But the two understood each other. "When we were looking at objects, what our eyes physically saw and what we came to perceive were exactly the same. And we would ask the same questions, have the same curiosity about things," Ive told *Time* magazine.

The products Jobs, Ive, and the Apple design team created changed Apple as a company. They helped Apple reestablish itself as a dominant technology and consumer product company. Those pivotal products include:

iMac: Introduced in 1998, the iMac was an unusual one-piece computer that sported a colorful translucent case. Apple launched an ad campaign featuring the phrase "Think Different" and photographs of creative individuals including Albert Einstein and Muppets creator Jim Henson.

iPod: The first generation of the iPod was released on October 23, 2001. The major innovation of the device was its small size. To achieve this, Apple used a 1.8-inch hard drive compared to the 2.5-inch drives common to MP3 players at that time. Before the end of 2001, more than one hundred thousand iPods were sold. The product, and the launch of Apple's iTunes Music Store, led to Apple becoming a major player in the music industry.

In the book *The Perfect Thing* by Steven Levy, Jobs said of the iPod, "If there was ever a product that catalyzed Apple's reason for being, it's this because it combines Apple's incredible technology base with Apple's legendary ease of use with Apple's awesome design. Those things come together and it's like, that's what we do. So if anybody is ever wondering, why is Apple on the Earth, I would hold this up as a good example."

iTunes: iTunes was an easy-to-use, aesthetically appealing music application and media library launched in 2001. By 2003, it also provided an easy gateway to an online music and media marketplace that Apple ran: the iTunes Store. The iTunes Store simplified the process and brought together music tracks from all the major labels. It also synced completely with the iPod, making buying and downloading music as simple as one click on your computer. By 2008, the iTunes Store would become the largest music retailer in the United States. The iTunes application, running on many different versions of Apple hardware, became the de facto computer jukebox for many consumers in the 2000s and also acted as a device manager.

iPhone: In 2005, Apple began work on the first iPhone, which made its debut on June 29, 2007. The iPhone launch led to long lines at Apple stores nationwide. The smartphone connected with consumers like no device before it. With the iPhone, consumers could make

The iPhone was a groundbreaking device that combined a phone with Internet accesss, GPS, and games. Apple sold 6.1 million units of the first-generation iPhone.

THE APPLE REVOLUTION: TEN KEY MOMENTS

1. A Friendship Begins: The seeds of Apple lay in the moment Steve Wozniak and Steve Jobs became friends and subsequently began working on designing and developing personal computers.

2. The Apple I: The Apple I was the first all-in-one computer that featured a keyboard and a monitor. It also came assembled, a first for computers at that time, which were all sold as kits that consumers assembled themselves.

3. The Macintosh: With the introduction of the Macintosh at the company's annual shareholders' meeting on January 24, 1984, pandemonium apparently ensued. At $2,495, the Macintosh was the first affordable computer to offer a graphical user interface, replacing text-based operating systems with an intuitive layout of folders and icons.

4. Steve Jobs Returns to Apple: In 1997, Apple was struggling against the competition and needed a boost. Jobs returned to Apple first as chairman of the board and then as chief executive officer.

5. The iMac: It became the best-selling personal computer in America. The iMac was a self-contained unit that included a computer screen, keyboard, and hard drive all in one sleek, attractive package. It also had

only one cord and minimal setup, which caught the attention of many first-time computer buyers.

6. The iPod: This portable music player enabled consumers to carry their entire libraries of music with them in one device.

7. Mac OS X: A breakthrough operating system, OS X was stable, fast, and had an ease of use that drew the interest of many new Mac users, who found themselves switching over from the Windows-based PC.

8. iTunes: Ease of use became a recurring theme for Apple in a number of its products. The iTunes Store, launched in 2003, made buying music as easy as one click. Consumers could legally download music for 99 cents a song.

9. The iPhone: Named *Time* magazine's "Invention of the Year" when it debuted in 2007, the iPhone forever altered the smartphone industry. The iPhone was a phone, music player, and mini computer all in one.

10. The iPad: It was not the first tablet computer, but when the iPad made its debut, again, it was an Apple product that made a big impact. The iPad became Apple's fastest-selling new product and revived the tablet computer market.

a call, text, search the Internet, and download hundreds of thousands of apps, or applications, that enabled users to find directions, play games, track their flights when traveling, log their workouts, and manage their schedules, among many other functions. *Time* magazine declared it "Invention of the Year" for 2007.

iPad: Tablet computers had been available for a while, but the iPad, released on April 3, 2010, combined myriad functions—such as Internet searches, taking

Apple became known worldwide for its innovation in launching beautifully designed, highly functional devices such as the iPad, the iPod, and the iPhone.

photos, filming videos, playing games, e-mailing, playing music, connecting on social media, and so much more.

APPLE STORES OPEN

In 2001, Apple stores began to pop up in shopping malls and retail centers around the United States. The stores were open, airy, and displayed Apple products on long tables, encouraging consumers to walk in, pick up a device, and begin to play with it. The stores also had well-trained staff

who were experts in all of Apple's computers and devices. They could walk a new user through the computer-buying experience, help an expert troubleshoot an issue, or introduce a new product. Each store also has a Genius Bar, a customer service counter where consumers can receive technical advice and guidance. As of June 2015, there are more than 454 Apple stores in sixteen countries and on three continents.

Chapter Five

LATER LIFE AND LEGACY

Steve Jobs and Steve Wozniak revolutionized the computer industry with the Apple I and the launch of Apple Computer, Inc. More than forty years later, the impact of their work is still felt not only in Apple products but throughout the computer industry.

JOBS FALLS ILL

In August 2004, Steve Jobs sent an e-mail to his employees at Apple to announce that he had been diagnosed with cancer. In his message he said, "I have some personal news that I need to share with you, and I wanted you to hear it directly from me. I have a very rare form of pancreatic cancer called an islet cell neuroendocrine tumor, which represents about 1 percent of the total

Steve Jobs introduced the ultra-slim MacBook Air at the 2008 MacWorld Expo. Because of his failing health, it would be his last public appearance.

cases of pancreatic cancer diagnosed each year, and can be cured by surgical removal if diagnosed in time (mine was). I will not require any chemotherapy or radiation treatments."

After surgery and throughout his recovery, Jobs remained dedicated to leading Apple and to introducing new products. Between 2004 and 2009, Apple launched new versions of the iPhone and iPod.

In January 2009, Jobs was absent from the annual Macworld event. In his place he sent Phil Schiller, Apple's marketing chief. He announced in a statement that his decision not to appear was not meant to set off a flurry of speculation about his health. However, he was still dealing with ongoing health issues. "Fortunately, after further testing, my doctors think they have found the cause—a hormone imbalance that has been 'robbing' me of the proteins

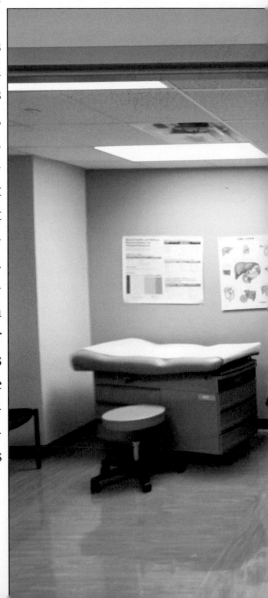

my body needs to be healthy." However, two weeks later, Jobs would take a medical leave from Apple when doctors discovered his health issues were more complex than they originally thought.

For the next five months, no other statements from Apple were issued about Jobs's health. But finally, in June, Apple announced that he had undergone a complete liver

James Eason, chief of transplantation at Methodist University Hospital, performed a liver transplant on Steve Jobs in an attempt to treat his cancer.

75

transplant in Tennessee. "At my request, the board of directors has granted me a medical leave of absence so I can focus on my health," Jobs said in a statement to the company. "I will continue as CEO and be involved in major strategic decisions for the company." A week later, Jobs was back to work at Apple.

But Jobs's health continued to decline and in August 2011, Jobs announced that he would be stepping down as CEO of Apple. He made the announcement in an e-mail to Apple employees, saying, "I have always said that if there ever came a day when I could no longer meet my duties and expectations as Apple's CEO, I would be the first to let you know. Unfortunately, that day has come." Jobs died on October 5, 2011, at the age of fifty-six, due to complications from pancreatic cancer.

REACTION TO JOBS'S DEATH

Jobs's death surprised many, partly because so little had been written about his illness. As word spread around the world, technology leaders and celebrities wrote passionate tributes to Jobs. They praised both his innovation as a technologist and his skills as a businessman:

The Apple website went dark the day of Jobs's death and displayed only an image of Jobs with his years of birth and death. He was fifty-six.

"Jobs gets a reputation for being a strong leader and for being brash. But to me he was always so kind, such a good friend."—Steve Wozniak, cofounder, Apple

"From the earliest days of Google, whenever Larry and I sought inspiration for vision and leadership, we needed to look no farther than Cupertino. Steve, your passion for excellence is felt by anyone who has ever touched an Apple product (including the MacBook I am writing this on right now). And I have witnessed it in person the few times we have met. On behalf of all of us at Google and more broadly in technology, you will be missed very much."—Sergey Brin, cofounder, Google

"Steve Jobs was a great friend as well as a trusted advisor. His legacy will extend far beyond the products he created or the businesses he built. It will be the millions of people he inspired, the lives he changed, and the culture he defined. Steve was such an 'original,' with a thoroughly creative, imaginative mind that defined an era. Despite all he accomplished, it feels like he was just getting started. With his passing the world has lost a rare original, Disney has lost a member of our family, and I have lost a great friend."—Bob Iger, president, Walt Disney Company

"Just learned the terrible news of Steve Jobs's passing. What an incredible, inspiring life. Changed the world in so many ways."—Chris Martin and Coldplay

"The world rarely sees someone who has had the profound impact Steve has had, the effects of which will be felt for many generations to come."—Bill Gates, cofounder, Microsoft

JOBS'S FAMILY AND HIS LEGACY

Jobs is survived by his wife, Laurene Powell Jobs, and his four children, Lisa Brennan-Jobs, Reed Jobs, Erin Jobs, and Eve Jobs. Powell Jobs has embraced several of her husband's philanthropic causes through the Steve P. Jobs Trust. Renamed the Laurene Powell Jobs Trust, the trust supports causes including immigration and urban education and numerous initiatives in Africa.

In Isaacson's biography of Jobs, the subject's own words conclude the book:

> Some people say, "Give the customers what they want." But that's not my approach. Our job is to figure out what they're going to want before they do. I think Henry Ford once said, "If I'd asked customers what they wanted, they would have told me, 'A faster horse!'" People don't know what they want until you show it to them. That's why I never rely on market research. Our task is to read things that are not yet on the page.
>
> What drove me? I think most creative people want to express appreciation for being able to take

STEVE JOBS AND STEVE WOZNIAK

advantage of the work that's been done by others before us. I didn't invent the language or mathematics I use. I make little of my own food, none of my own clothes. Everything I do depends on other members of our species and the shoulders that we stand on. And a lot of us want to contribute something back to our species and to add something to the flow. It's about trying to express something in the only way that most of us know how—because we can't write Bob Dylan songs or Tom Stoppard plays. We try to use the talents we do have to express our deep feelings, to show our appreciation of all the contributions that came before us, and to add something to that flow. That's what has driven me.

APPLE AFTER JOBS

During Jobs's multiple medical leaves, Tim Cook, the company's chief operating officer, took over. When Jobs stepped down from Apple, Cook was announced as the new chief executive officer. When Jobs passed away, Cook said in a letter to employees that "Apple has lost a visionary and creative genius, and the world has lost an amazing human being. We will honor his memory by dedicating ourselves to continuing the work he loved so much."

JOBS AND WOZNIAK: IMMORTALIZED ON SCREEN AND IN PRINT

Jobs and Wozniak's success story has found its way onto screens both large and small in a variety of TV movies and feature films.

Pirates of Silicon Valley was a made-for-television movie that aired in 2009. Wozniak thought the film captured the essence of his and Jobs's rise to fame. He told Business Insider that *"Pirates of Silicon Valley* was intriguing, interesting. I loved watching it."

But not every biographical project hits the right tone or gets the facts straight. In Wozniak's opinion, *Jobs*, a feature film starring actor Ashton Kutcher as Steve Jobs and actor and comedian Josh Gad as Steve Wozniak, failed to deliver a story that was based on the real facts of Jobs's and Wozniak's lives. Wozniak himself gave the film a negative review on the website Gizmodo. In his analysis, he wrote, "I felt bad for many people I know well who were portrayed wrongly in their interactions with Jobs and the company." He added in an interview with the *Los Angeles Times* that a key scene in the film is wrong. "Steve is lecturing me about where computers could go, when it was the other way around. Steve never created a great computer. In that period, he had failure after failure after failure. He had an incredible vision, but he didn't have the ability to execute on it. I would be surprised if the movie portrays the truth."

Kutcher responded to Wozniak's statements negatively, telling *The Hollywood Reporter*: "A couple things you have to understand. One, Steve Wozniak is being paid by another movie studio to help support their Steve

Steve Wozniak continues to speak around the world at events, including the opening of Telcel Digital Village in Mexico City, Mexico.

Jobs film, so he's gonna have an opinion that is connected to that, somewhat. Two, the biggest criticism that I've ultimately heard is that he wanted it to be represented— his contribution to Apple—fairly. And, in all fairness, the movie's called *Jobs*. And it's about Steve Jobs and the legacy of Steve Jobs, and so I think it focuses more . . . on what his contribution to Apple was."

Kutcher also criticized Wozniak for not making himself available for consulting or even conversations about his and Jobs's lives.

Before his death, Jobs invited Walter Isaacson, a former managing editor of *Time* magazine and a former CEO of CNN, to write his exclusive biography. The result was *Steve Jobs*, a book based on more than forty interviews with Jobs over a two-year period. Jobs encouraged Isaacson to also talk to family members, friends,

MOST REVEALING QUOTES
FROM STEVE JOBS

Over more than forty interviews, Jobs shared many details of his life with Walter Isaacson, whom he gave complete editorial control when crafting Jobs's biography. Some of the most fascinating facts to come from the book include:

On living with an illness: "Living with a disease like this, and all the pain, constantly reminds you of your own mortality, and that can do strange things to your brain if you're not careful. You don't make plans more than a year out, and that's bad. You need to force yourself to plan as if you will live for many years."

On religion: "The juice goes out of Christianity when it becomes too based on faith rather than living like Jesus or seeing the world as Jesus saw it . . . I think different religions are different doors to the same house. Sometimes I think the house exists, and sometimes I don't. It's the great mystery."

On his colleagues: "I've learned over the years that when you have really good people you don't have to baby them. By expecting them to do great things, you can get them to do great things. The original Mac team taught me that A-plus players like to work together, and they don't like it if you tolerate B work."

On the social media craze: "There's a temptation in our networked age to think that ideas can be developed by e-mail and iChat. That's crazy. Creativity comes from spontaneous meetings, from random discussions. You run into someone, you ask what they're doing, you say, 'Wow,' and soon you're cooking up all sorts of ideas."

adversaries, competitors, and colleagues. Jobs cooperated with the writing of the book, and he asked for no control over what was written and did not ask to read it before it was published. He also encouraged the people he knew to speak honestly about him and their experiences in working with or for him. In the book, Jobs is open about his success and his failures, both in business and in his personal life. The book sold more than 379,000 copies in the United States in its first week, making it the top-selling book in the country.

Isaacson's book has been optioned as a feature film and the script is to be written by Aaron Sorkin, who wrote the script for the film *The Social Network* and is well-known for having created and written the hit TV show *The West Wing*. Wozniak is said to be involved in consulting on the film.

Wozniak also spent time writing his story in an autobiography titled *iWoz: From Computer Geek to Cult*

Icon: How I Invented the Personal Computer, Co-Founded Apple, and Had Fun Doing It. Wozniak, in an interview with the *San Jose Mercury News*, has said what he wants his legacy to be: "Being a good father. And, I'd like to be remembered for having been a good person who had business success who didn't step on people's toes and who didn't run over them and treat them badly and get into arguments over what's right and wrong. And I'd like to be remembered for having designed some really great computers that helped inspire this whole computer revolution."

Timeline

August 11, 1950: Steve Wozniak is born.

February 24, 1955: Steve Jobs is born.

1971: Steve Wozniak and Steve Jobs meet.

March 1976: Wozniak and Jobs present the Apple I to the Homebrew Computer Club.

April 1, 1976: Wozniak and Jobs establish their company, Apple Computer.

January 3, 1977: Apple Computer, Inc., is incorporated.

April 16, 1977: The Apple II is introduced to consumers at the West Coast Computer Faire.

1978: The Apple II becomes the first mass-market personal computer.

December 12, 1980: Apple goes public; Wozniak and Jobs become multi-millionaires.

February 7, 1981: Wozniak and his then-fiancée Candice Clark are injured in a plane crash.

1985: Jobs quits Apple and starts NeXT, Inc., a new computer company.

1986: Wozniak earns a bachelor's degree in electrical engineering and computer science. Jobs buys Lucasfilm's Computer Division and later renames it Pixar Animation Studios.

1987: Wozniak stops working full-time at Apple and launches a new company, CL-9.

1997: Steve Jobs returns to Apple.

1998: The iMac is released and quickly becomes the best-selling personal computer of the time.

2001: Wozniak founds Wheels of Zeus.

March 2001: The OS X operating system is released.

October 2001: The iPod is introduced.

2003: iTunes launches and changes the way people buy music.

August 2004: Jobs announces in an e-mail to his employees at Apple that he has been diagnosed with cancer.

2006: Jobs sells Pixar Animation Studios to Disney.

September 2006: Wozniak publishes his autobiography, *iWoz: From Computer Geek to Cult Icon: How I Invented the Personal Computer, Co-Founded Apple, and Had Fun Doing It*.

June 29, 2007: The iPhone goes on sale. That same month, Jobs returns to Apple.

September 2007: Wozniak joins Scottevest as an advisory board member.

January 2009: Jobs takes a leave of absence from Apple and later undergoes a liver transplant.

February 2009: Wozniak joins Fusion-io as its chief scientist.

January 27, 2010: The iPad goes on sale.

August 2011: Jobs announces that he will resign from Apple due to his failing health.

October 5, 2011: Jobs dies at the age of fifty-six.

June 2015: The Apple Watch is released. It is Apple's first new product release since Jobs's death.

Glossary

amnesia A loss of memory.

anterograde Affecting memories of new information after a patient has suffered a shock or seizure.

app Short for "application." Software that enables a computer to perform certain tasks.

board of directors A body of elected or appointed members who jointly oversee the activities of a company or organization.

breadboarding Making an experimental base for prototyping electronic devices.

Buddhist A person who practice Buddhism, an eastern religion and philosophy that arose in India but has followers everywhere.

consumer A person who buys goods and services.

embankment A wall or bank of earth or stone built to prevent flooding.

epicenter A point where an earthquake or underground explosion originates.

fracture A break in a bone.

ham radio An amateur radio used by electronic hobbyists.

hiatus A pause or gap in a series or series of events.

humanities An academic discipline that studies human culture.

immigrant A person who comes from one country to another to live or work.

innovation The act or process of introducing new ideas, devices, or methods.

liberal Believing that government should provide equal opportunity and equality for all.

machinist A person who uses machine tools to make or modify metal parts.

mass market The market for goods that are produced in large quantities.

MP3 A device for playing digital audio files.

operating system Software that manages computer hardware and software.

programming language A formal language designed to communicate instructions to a machine, particularly a computer.

prototype An example of a product that has not yet been tested.

shareholder Someone who owns stock in a company.

voltmeter An instrument used for measuring the voltage, or electrical current, between two points in an electric circuit.

For More Information

American Society of Engineering Education
1818 N. Street, NW, Suite 600
Washington, DC 20036-2479
(202) 331-3500
Website: http://www.asee.org
The American Society for Engineering Education
is a nonprofit organization of individuals and
institutions committed to furthering education in
engineering and engineering technology.

Association for Computing Machinery (ACM)
2 Penn Plaza, Suite 701
New York, NY 10121-0701
(800) 342-6626
Website: http://www.acm.org
ACM, the world's largest educational and scientific computing society, delivers resources that
advance computing as a science and a profession.

Association for Women in Computing (AWC)
P.O. Box 2768
Oakland, CA 94602
nfo@awc-hq.org
Website: http://www.awc-hq.org/home.html

AWC is one of the first professional organizations
for women in computing. The organization is
dedicated to promoting the advancement of
women in the computing professions.

Association of Information Technology Professionals (AITP)
1120 Route 73, Suite 200
Mount Laurel, NJ 08054-5113
(800) 224-9371
Website: http://www.aitp.org
AITP is the leading worldwide society of information technology business professionals and the
community of knowledge for the current and
next generation of leaders.

Canadian Association of Computer Science/Associ-
ation d'Informatique Canadienne (CACS)
Department of Computer Science
University of Calgary
2500 University Drive NW
Calgary AB T2N 1N4
Canada
(403) 220-8497

Website: http://www.cpsc.ucalgary.ca/~barker
CACS provides resources and information to
    professionals and students interested in further
    developing their skills and knowledge of com-
    puter science.

Canadian Information Processing Society (CIPS)
5090 Explorer Drive, Suite 801
Mississauga, Ontario L4W 4T9
Canada
(905) 602-1370
CIPS works to strengthen the Canadian IT industry
    by establishing standards and sharing best prac-
    tices for the benefit of individual IT professionals
    and the industry as a whole.

Digital Promise
1731 Connecticut Avenue NW, 4th Floor
Washington, DC 20009
(202) 450-3675
Website: http://www.digitalpromise.org
Digital Promise supports research and development
    to provide Americans with the knowledge and
    skills needed to compete in the global economy.

International Academy of Digital
    Arts and Science
22 West 21st Street, 7th Floor
New York, NY 10010
(212) 675-4890
Website: http://www.iadas.net
The International Academy of Digital Arts and
    Sciences was founded in 1998 to help drive the
    creative, technical, and professional progress of
    the Internet and evolving forms of interactive
    media.

Internet Society
1775 Wiehle Avenue, Suite 201
Reston, VA 20190-5108
(703) 439-2120
Website: https://www.internetsociety.org
The Internet Society's purpose is to promote the
    open development, evolution, and use of the
    Internet for the benefit of all people throughout
    the world.

World Wide Web Consortium (W3C)
(718) 260-9447

The World Wide Web Consortium (W3C) is an international community in which member organizations work together to develop web standards.

WEBSITES

Because of the changing number of Internet links, Rosen Publishing has developed an online list of websites related to the subject of this book. This site is updated regularly. Please use this link to access this list:

http://www.rosenlinks.com/TP/Jobs

For Further Reading

Blumenthal, Karen. *Steve Jobs: The Man Who Thought Different*. New York, NY: Square Fish/ Macmillan Publishers USA, 2012.

Brandt, Richard L. *The Google Guys: Inside the Brilliant Minds of Google Founders Larry Page and Sergey Brin*. New York, NY: Portfolio Trade, 2011.

Brandt, Richard L. *One Click: Jeff Bezos and the Rise of Amazon.com*. New York, NY: Portfolio Trade, 2012.

Buckley, A. M. *Pixar: The Company and Its Founders*. Edina, MN: ABDO Publishers, 2011.

Chmielewski, Gary T. *How Did That Get to My House? Internet*. Nampa, ID: Cherry Creek Publishing, 2013.

Cindrich, Sharon, and Ali Douglass. *A Smart Girl's Guide to the Internet*. Middleton, WI: American Girl, 2009.

D'Epiro, Peter. *The Book of Firsts: 150 World-Changing People and Events from Caesar Augustus to the Internet*. Harpswell, ME: Anchor Publishing, 2010.

Duggan, Michael. *iPad Action Gaming for Teens*. Independence, KY: Cengage Learning PTR, 2013.

Funk, Joe. *Cool Careers in Interactive Development: Hot Jobs in Video Games*. New York, NY: Scholastic, 2010.

Grinapol, Corinne. *Internet Biographies: Reed Hastings and Netflix*. New York, NY: Rosen Publishing Group, 2013.

Harris, Ashley Rae. *Microsoft: The Company and Its Founders*. Edina, MN: ABDO Publishers, 2012.

Kahney, Leander. *Jony Ive: The Genius Behind Apple's Greatest Products*. New York, NY: Penguin Group/Portfolio, 2013.

Landau, Jennifer. *Jeff Bezos and Amazon* (Internet Biographies). New York, NY: Rosen Publishing Group, 2012.

Lashinsky, Adam. *Inside Apple: How America's Most Admired—and Secretive—Company Really Works*. New York, NY: Hachette Book Group/Business Plus, 2012.

Lengyel, Eric. *Mathematics for 3D Game Programming and Computer Graphics*. Independence, KY: Cengage Learning PTR, 2011.

Levy, Stephen, and Chris Anderson. *WIRED: Steve Jobs, Revolutionary*. Seattle, WA: *Wired*/Amazon Digital Services, Inc., 2011.

Lusted, Marcia Amidon. *Netflix: The Company and Its Founders*. Edina, MN: ABDO Publishers, 2012.

Marcovitz, Hal. *Online Gaming and Entertainment* (Issues in the Digital Age). San Diego, CA: Referencepoint Press, 2011.

Purcell, Karen. *Unlocking Your Brilliance: Smart Strategies for Women to Thrive in Science, Technology, Engineering and Math*. Austin, TX: Greenleaf Book Group Press, 2012.

Ripley, Amanda. *The Smartest Kids in the World: And How They Got That Way*. New York, NY: Simon and Schuster, 2013.

Robinson, Tom. *Jeff Bezos: Amazon.com Architect*. Minneapolis, MN: ABDO Publishing Company, 2009.

Sande, Warren, and Carter Sande. *Hello World! Computer Programming for Kids and Other Beginners*. Shelter Island, NY: Manning Publications, 2009.

Swanson, Jennifer, and Glen Mullaly. *How the Internet Works*. North Mankato, MN: Child's World Publishing, 2011.

Vogelstein, Fred. *Dogfight: How Apple and Google Went to War and Started a Revolution*. New York,

NY: Sarah Crichton Books, 2013.

Wagner, Tony. *Creating Innovators: The Making of Young People Who Will Change the World*. New York, NY: Scribner, 2012.

Wittekind, Erika. *Amazon.com: The Company and Its Founders*. Edina, MN: ABDO Publishers, 2012.

Bibliography

"The Apple Revolution: 10 Key Moments." *Time*, January 23, 2009. Retrieved June 22, 2015 (http://content.time.com/time/specials/packages/article/0,28804,1873486_1873491_1873530,00.html).

Beuter, Alison. "One-on-One with 'Woz': Steve Wozniak Talks Steve Jobs." *Milwaukee Business Journal*, June 27, 2014. Retrieved June 22, 2015 (http://www.bizjournals.com/milwaukee/blog/2014/06/one-on-one-with-woz-steve-wozniak-talks-steve-jobs.html).

Bort, Julie. "Apple Cofounder Steve Wozniak Gives Some Great Advice For Your Career." Business Insider, April 16, 2013. Retrieved June 22, 2015 (http://www.businessinsider.com/apple-cofounder-steve-wozniak-has-some-great-advice-for-your-career-2013-4).

Bort, Julie. "Hewlett Packard Could Have Been Apple If Not For 5 Bad Decisions." Business Insider, February 1, 2013. Retrieved June 17, 2015 (http://www.businessinsider.com/woz-begged-hp-to-make-the-apple-pc-2013-2).

Childs, Dan, and Kevin Dolak. "Steve Jobs' Pancreatic Cancer: A Timeline." ABC News, October 6, 2011. Retrieved June 23, 2015 (http://abcnews.

go.com/Health/CancerPreventionAndTreat-
ment/steve-jobs-pancreatic-cancer-timeline/sto-
ry?id=14681812).

Eadicicco, Lisa. "One of Apple's Earliest Employees Describes the First Time Steve Jobs Met His
Genius Cofounder Steve Wozniak." Business
Insider, December 8, 2014. Retrieved June 18,
2015 (https://lockerdome.com/businessinsider.
com/7219613868106004).

Entis, Laura. "Former Apple CEO John Sculley: This
Is What Made Steve Jobs a Genius." Entrepreneur.
com, March 4, 2015. Retrieved June 22, 2015
(http://www.entrepreneur.com/video/243191).

Flippo, Chet. "Once an Electronics Nerd, Apple
Computer Whiz Stephen Wozniak Now Finds
Life Is a Festival." *People*, May 30, 1983. Retrieved
June 18, 2015 (http://www.people.com/people/
archive/article/0,,20085132,00.html).

Hendricks, Drew. "6 $25 Billion Companies That
Started in a Garage." *Inc.*, July 24, 2014. Retrieved
June 18, 2015 (http://www.inc.com/drew-
hendricks/6-25-billion-companies-that-started-
in-a-garage.html).

Isaacson, Walter. *Steve Jobs*. New York, NY: Simon and Schuster, 2013.

Kane, Yukari Iwatani, and Geoffrey A. Fowler. "Steven Paul Jobs, 1955–2011." *Wall Street Journal*, October 6, 2011. Retrieved June 16, 2015 (http://www.wsj.com/articles/SB1000142405270230444780457641075321081190).

Karkaria, Urvaksh. "Wozniak: 'I Begged HP to Make the Apple I. Five Times They Turned Me Down.'" *Atlanta Business Journal*, January 31, 2013. Retrieved June 17, 2015 (http://www.bizjournals.com/atlanta/blog/atlantech/2013/01/woz-i-begged-h-p-to-make-the-apple-1.html).

Kelly, Heather. "5 ways the iPhone changed our lives." CNN, June 30, 2012. Retrieved June 16, 2015 (http://www.cnn.com/2012/06/28/tech/mobile/iphone-5-years-anniversary).

Krasny, Jill. "Ex-Apple CEO John Sculley on Steve Jobs: 'We Were Meant to Be a Team.'" *Inc.*, December 22, 2014. Retrieved June 22, 2015 (http://www.inc.com/jill-krasny/john-sculley-steve-jobs-meant-to-be-a-team.html).

La Monica, Paul R. "Disney buys Pixar." January 25, 2006. Retrieved June 23, 2015 (http://money.cnn.

com/2006/01/24/news/companies/disney_pixar_
deal).

Lewis, Keith. "Education Issue Extra: Advice from
Steve Wozniak." Craft Council, November 14,
2013. Retrieved June 22, 2015 (http://
craftcouncil.org/post/education-issue-extra-
advice-steve-wozniak#sthash.e5vTET5q.dpuf).

Lisy, Brandon. "Steve Wozniak on Apple, the Computer Revolution, and Working with Steve Jobs."
Bloomberg, December 4, 2014. Retrieved June
18, 2015 (http://www.bloomberg.com/bw/
articles/2014-12-04/apple-steve-wozniak-on-the-
early-years-with-steve-jobs).

Moon, Peter. "Three Minutes with Steve Wozniak."
ABC News, July 20, 2007. Retrieved June 18,
2015 (http://abcnews.go.com/Technology/
PCWorld/story?id=3396207).

Purdy, Kevin. "How Apple Co-founder Steve
Wozniak Gets Things Done." Lifehacker.com,
April 22, 2009. Retrieved June 22, 2015 (http://
lifehacker.com/5222989/how-apple-co-founder-
steve-wozniak-gets-things-done).

"Steve Jobs: Adopted child who never met his
biological father." *Telegraph*, October 6, 2011.

Retrieved June 17, 2015 (http://www.telegraph.
co.uk/technology/steve-jobs/8811345/Steve-Jobs-
adopted-child-who-never-met-his-biological-
father.html).

"Steve Wozniak Biography." Biography.com.
Retrieved June 17, 2015 (http://www.biography.
com/people/steve-wozniak-9537334).

"Steve Wozniak Biography." The Famous People.
Retrieved June 17, 2015 (http://www.thefamous-
people.com/profiles/steve-wozniak-5160.php).

Stix, Harriet. "A UC Berkeley Degree Is Now the
Apple of Steve Wozniak's Eye." *Los Angeles
Times*, May 14, 1986. Retrieved June 17, 2015
(http://articles.latimes.com/1986-05-14/news/
vw-5389_1_steve-wozniak).

Wolfson, Jill, and John Leyba. "An Interview with
Steve Wozniak." Tech Museum of Innovation
(https://www.thetech.org/exhibits/online/
revolution/wozniak/i_a.html).

Index